First published in Belgium and Holland by Clavis Uitgeverij, Hasselt – Amsterdam, 2014
Copyright © 2014, Clavis Uitgeverij

English translation from the Dutch by Clavis Publishing Inc. New York
Copyright © 2017 for the English language edition: Clavis Publishing Inc. New York

Visit us on the web at www.clavisbooks.com

Doctors and What They Do written and illustrated by Liesbet Slegers
Original title: *De dokter*
Translated from the Dutch by Clavis Publishing

ISBN 978-1-60537-322-5

This book was printed in April 2017 at Publikum d.o.o., Slavka Rodica 6, Belgrade, Serbia

First Edition
10 9 8 7 6 5 4 3 2 1

Clavis Publishing supports the First Amendment and celebrates the right to read

Doctors
and What They Do
Liesbet Slegers

Clavis

NEW YORK

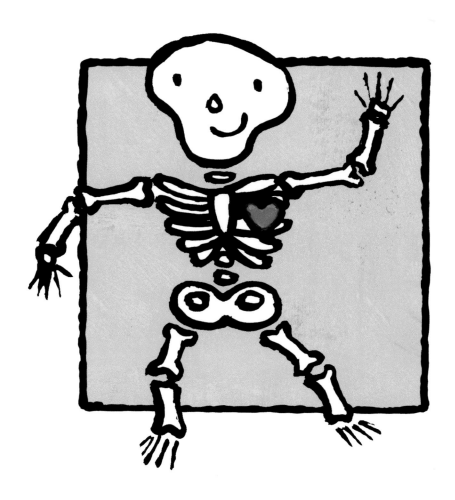

It's not nice being sick. To get better again, you can visit a doctor.

A doctor knows a lot about the body.

The doctor figures out what's wrong and checks if you need medicine.

But you can also visit the doctor when you're feeling good.

Then the doctor examines your entire body and tells you
how you can stay healthy and fit.

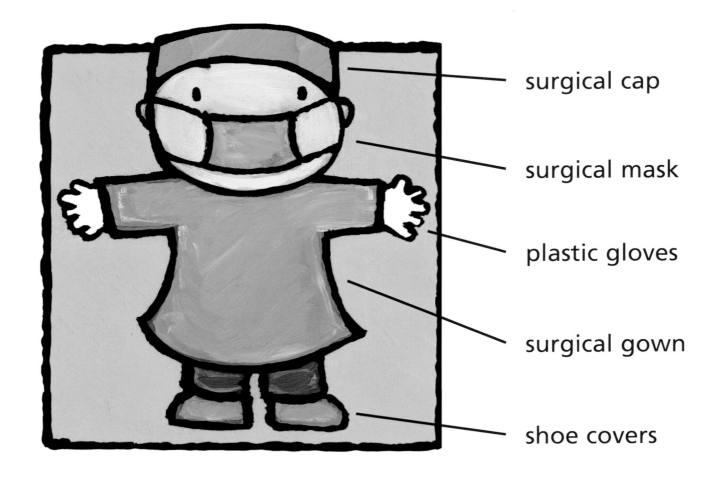

surgical cap

surgical mask

plastic gloves

surgical gown

shoe covers

The doctor wears a long, white coat over her regular clothes. The doctor's coat has pockets so she can carry a pen, paper, a stethoscope and many other things with her. A doctor who performs surgeries wears special clothes: a surgical gown, a surgical cap, plastic gloves, a surgical mask and shoe covers. That way, bacteria don't stand a chance!
(Bacteria are teeny-weeny animals that can make you sick.)

long, white
doctor's
coat

doctor's bag

The doctor examines her patients on the examination table.
She uses a stethoscope (for listening to the heart and the lungs),
a blood pressure monitor, a light to look into the ears and a tongue
depressor to look into the throat. Once the doctor knows
what's wrong, she will also need things to make the patient better
again: a pair of tweezers for removing a splinter, disinfectant,
sterile cotton wads, a pair of scissors, bandages, a syringe.
Or she prescribes medicines and explains how you should use them.
She checks if you've grown with a stadiometer. The scale shows
how much you weigh. She keeps track of everything she knows
about a patient on her computer.

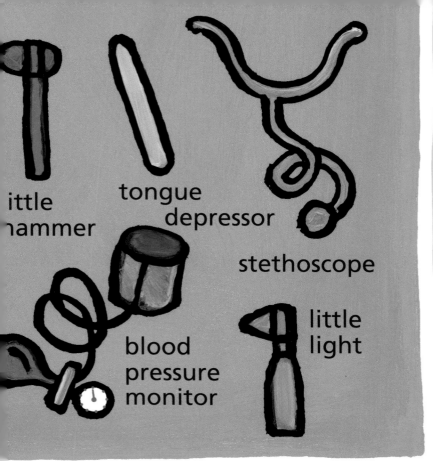

little hammer

tongue depressor

stethoscope

blood pressure monitor

little light

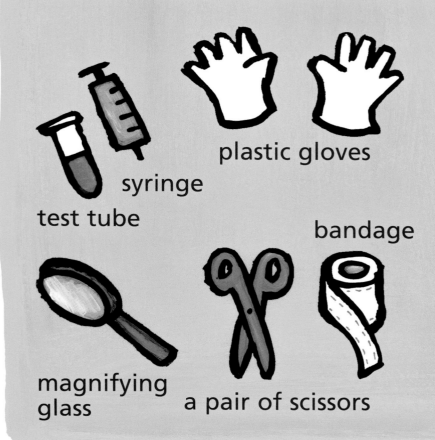

test tube

syringe

plastic gloves

bandage

magnifying glass

a pair of scissors

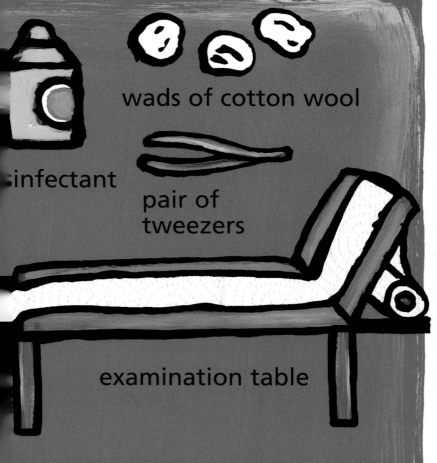

wads of cotton wool

disinfectant

pair of tweezers

examination table

thermometer

scale

stadiometer

21,31

It's crowded in the doctor's waiting room.

A little boy and his daddy are next.

"Hello, Brad, I haven't seen you in a long time.

My, you've grown! What's the matter?" the doctor asks kindly.

"I'm sick," Brad says shyly.

"Brad has a fever and has to cough a lot," Daddy says.

"His ears hurt too."

"I will take a look," the doctor says,

"so I can make you better again quickly."

Daddy helps Brad take off his clothes.

That way, the doctor can listen to his chest with her stethoscope.

"I can hear your heart beating really well. That's a beautiful sound,"

the doctor says with a smile. "Take a deep breath, Brad,

so I can listen to your lungs."

Brad coughs.

Then the doctor uses a special light to look into Brad's ears.

"Now I'm going to feel your belly," the doctor says.

"This might tickle a bit." She examines his stomach with her hands.

Is everything all right in there? "You have a healthy belly, Brad,"

she says, "but the fever is making you feel warm.

Look, this is a tongue depressor. Open your mouth for me,

so I can take a look at your throat. Very good, Brad.

There, now we will make you all better."

"I'll prescribe some medicine," the doctor says.
"You'll take three spoonfuls every day. That way, you'll feel better soon. You shouldn't go to school for a couple of days, because you need to rest."
Daddy and Brad go home again.
"Bye, Doctor!" Brad says happily.
"Thank you," Daddy says.

It's someone else's turn. A mommy enters with her baby.

The child isn't sick but needs a shot.

It protects the baby against nasty diseases.

"Hello, little girl," the doctor says. "Just a quick shot.

It will be over in a jiffy. My, you're brave!"

The mommy comforts her baby. It's no big deal.

Soon, the little girl will come back for another shot.

A little book shows which shots she still needs.

The doctor records the shot she just gave her.

The doctor gets an urgent call. A child has been brought
to the hospital. The doctor goes immediately to the emergency room.
That's where patients go when they need help really quickly – after
an accident, for example. It's very busy in the emergency room.
A lot of people are walking around. In the distance, you can hear
an ambulance. Someone passes by in a wheelchair. And there's
a woman with a big belly. Maybe her baby will be born soon!

"Hello, my dear. What's your name?" the doctor asks.

"And can you tell me what happened?"

The girl is crying. "My name is Lola and I fell off my bike," she says.

"My arm hurts a lot."

The doctor examines the arm and checks to see if the girl

is hurt somewhere else too.

"The nurse will take a special picture of that arm," the doctor says,
"so that I can see the bones inside it. Don't be scared, Lola.
Taking a picture doesn't hurt."
The nurse is already here. Mommy can come along too.
"Keep your arm very still on the table. That's good, Lola!"
The picture is ready. The doctor shows it to her on the computer.
"Look, there is a small crack in your bone." The doctor points.
"The nurse will put your arm in a cast. It will soon be healed."

Lola gets to pick the color of her cast.

"You are such a brave girl," the doctor says.

"And you really have a nice cast! In a few weeks' time,

the cast can come off again."

Lola and her mommy go back home. Lola smiles.

And when children go home happy, the doctor is happy too.

A **doctor** can work as a family doctor,
but he or she can also do other things.

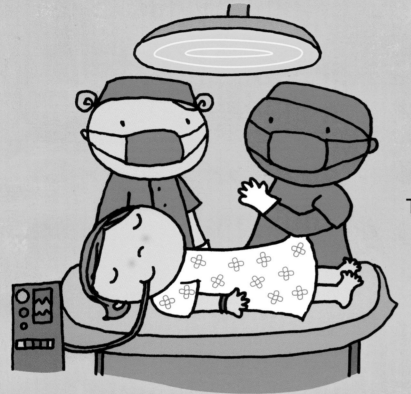

Some doctors perform
a lot of **surgeries**.
They get help from **nurses**.

There are doctors that know
everything about **babies
inside bellies**.
They give the mommies advice.
Look, this baby is already really big!